KU-453-161

# MY FRIEND is Blind

BY NICOLA EDWARDS

Chrysalis Children's Books

First published in the UK in 2004 by
Chrysalis Children's Books
An imprint of Chrysalis Books Group
The Chrysalis Building, Bramley Road
London W10 6SP

ISBN 1 84458 098 9

British Library Cataloguing in Publication Data for this book is available
from the British Library.

**Editorial Manager:** Joyce Bentley
**Editors:** Joe Fullman and Jon Richards
**Designers:** Ed Simkins and Ben Ruocco
**Photographer:** Michael Wicks
**Picture researcher:** Lorna Ainger
**Illustrations:** Hardlines Ltd

Produced by Tall Tree Ltd

**Consultant:** Myrtle Robinson, Royal National Institute for the Blind
*The Royal National Institute for the Blind is a UK charity that offers information, support and advice to people with sight problems. To find out more about the charity, contact the office listed on page 31.*

The photographer, author and publishers would like to thank Philippa Phillips, Hannah Matin, Sharon Keya, Sima Matin, Miles Gray and David Schueler.

**Picture acknowledgments:**
Alamy: Bill Bachmann 15br
Corbis: Tom Stewart 19r
Getty Images: Jonathan Nourok 6l
Courtesy The Guide Dogs for the Blind Association: 23r
Science Photo Library: 21r, Mauro Fermariello 21r, Sue Ford 9r, Cristina Pedrazzini 29br
Still Pictures: Adrian Arbib 8l

Printed in China

10 9 8 7 6 5 4 3 2 1

# Contents

*Words in **bold** are explained in the glossary on page 30.*

# My friend Hannah

*Hannah has been partially sighted since she was a toddler.*

Hello! My name's Sharon and this is my friend Hannah. We've been friends for a long time. We live near each other and we both go to the same school. Hannah and I like a lot of the same things. We both want to be journalists when we're older and at the moment we're helping to write the school magazine.

*Sharon (left) and Hannah are best friends and enjoy making each other laugh.*

Hannah has a problem with her eyesight and she is registered as blind (see below), although she can see a little out of her right eye. In fact, the vision in her right eye is called **tunnel vision** because she cannot see too well to either side. I used to think that if someone was blind, they couldn't see anything at all. Since I got to know Hannah, I have learned that there are lots of different types of blindness, or **visual impairment**. Being visually impaired can mean that a person has a slight problem with seeing, or that he or she cannot see anything at all.

## BLINDNESS FACTS

### BLIND AND PARTIALLY SIGHTED

A person is considered to be blind if they cannot read the top line of an eye chart from a distance of three metres or less. A person who cannot read the top line from a distance of six metres or less is **partially sighted**.

# What is sight?

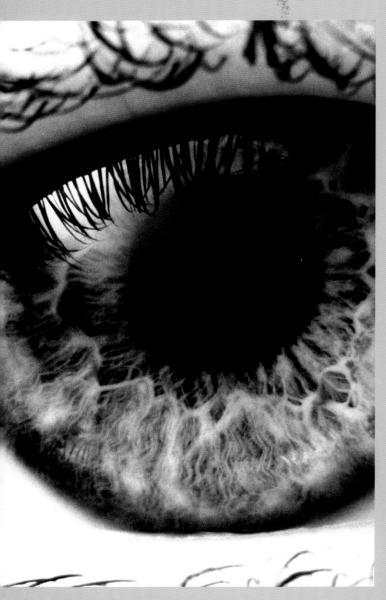

Each human eye is made up of different parts which work together to allow a person to see light, colour, patterns and shapes, and to notice movements and judge how far away things are. Cyclists, for example, use their eyes to work out how far they are from other road users and to note if there are any obstacles in their path. A complicated system of **nerves** sends signals from the eyes to the brain. The brain interprets these signals as the picture the person sees.

The eye is covered by a tough outer layer. The see-through part of this layer at the front of the eye is called the **cornea**. Behind the cornea is the ring-shaped **iris**, the coloured part of the eye. In the middle of the iris is a hole called the **pupil**, which can become bigger or smaller to let more or less light into the eye. Behind the pupil is the curved **lens**. Light shines through the cornea, the pupil, the lens and the middle of the eye onto the **retina**, at the back of the eye.

*At the centre of your eye is the black pupil which gets bigger or smaller to let more or less light into the eye. Around this is the coloured iris.*

When light shines onto the retina it causes the nerves to send signals, which travel along the **optic nerve** to the brain. The area of the brain that processes these signals and works out what they mean is called the **visual cortex**.

If there is a problem with one or more of the parts that make up the eye, this can cause visual impairment. Problems with sight can also occur if parts of the brain do not interpret the signals they are sent correctly.

*Rays of light enter your eye to cast an image on the retina at the back of the eye. Rays of light cross over when they enter the eye, so the picture on the back is actually upside down! Your brain then turns this image the right way up.*

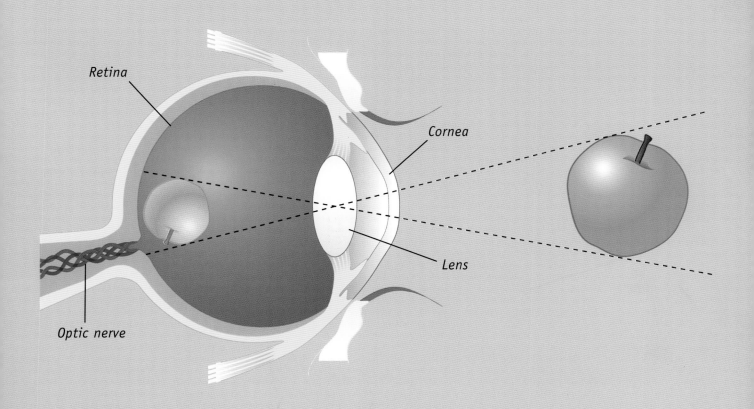

Retina

Cornea

Lens

Optic nerve

# Problems with sight

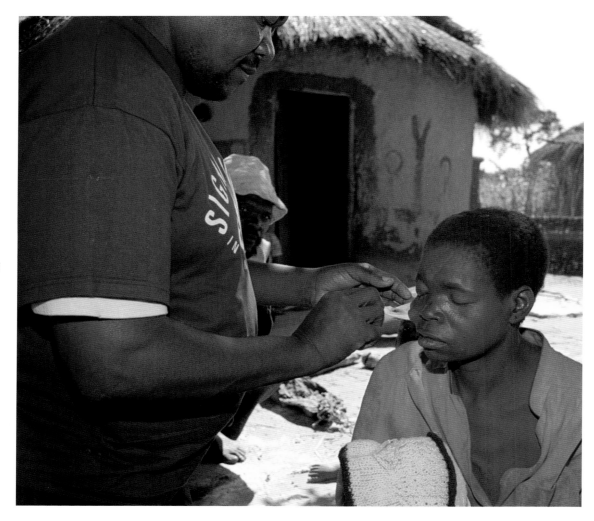

*This person is suffering from an eye condition called trachoma, which is caused by unhygienic living conditions.*

The causes of visual impairment are varied. A baby may be born with sight problems if parts of the eyes haven't formed correctly. Sometimes this happens because of an illness which the baby's mother developed while the baby was still forming inside her.

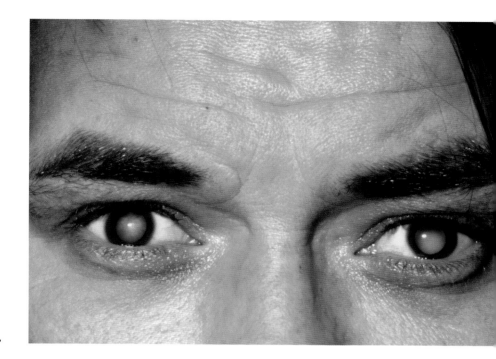

*This person's visual impairment has been caused by cataracts, or cloudy patches on the eye's lens. Surgeons can operate on patients to remove cataracts.*

Some diseases can affect the eyes and cause visual impairment. For example, a disease called macular degeneration affects the retina and an eye disease called glaucoma causes pressure to build up inside the eye. The chances of developing these diseases increase with age, so not many children are affected by them.

People who live in poorer, **developing countries** are more at risk from blindness-causing diseases that spread where living conditions are unhygienic and where there is a lack of clean water.

Each person with a visual impairment has his or her own experience of sight. Someone who is blind, for example, while not being able to see things clearly, may be able to see light and shadows.

# BLINDNESS FACTS

## STATISTICS

About two million people in the UK have a sight problem or visual impairment. Roughly half of these people are registered (or qualify to be registered) as blind or partially sighted. Each person's sight loss is different and no two people experience it in exactly the same way.

# At Hannah's house

*Hannah uses a CCTV device, a machine which magnifies print and makes it easier for her to read.*

Hannah's family has just moved to a new house. The first thing I noticed was that it's much tidier than my house! No one leaves things lying around on the floor in case Hannah trips over them.

Hannah says that she has a map in her head of where everything is, so it's important that everything stays in the same place. All the furniture has soft, padded edges, just in case Hannah walks into anything.

Hannah showed me how she can tell the difference between a can of beans and a can of peaches by the weight of the cans and the sounds they make when she shakes them. She chooses which clothes to wear by how they feel as well as how they look. Hannah does use some special pieces of equipment, such as her computer, to help her, but there are simple things that help, too. In the bathroom, her toothbrush has an elastic band round it, so that it feels different from everyone else's.

*When Hannah uses the stairs, she counts each step so she knows when she's reached the top or the bottom.*

## BLINDNESS FACTS

### HELPFUL PRODUCTS

Many products have been specially developed to help people with sight problems, including:
- coin holders, to make it easier to find the right money when paying for something
- globes that can be read by touch
- portable computers with Braille keyboards
- telephones with large buttons that are easier to see
- footballs filled with ball bearings that rattle when they move
- watches and clocks that can be read by touching them

# Learning Braille

Hannah is learning **Braille** at the moment. We've learned about Braille in school. It's a system that uses patterns of raised dots on paper to represent letters and punctuation marks. People who are visually impaired can read the dots by running their fingers over them (see page 28). Hannah showed me the different patterns of dots that stand for each letter of the alphabet. It looks a bit complicated to me, but Hannah says her Braille teacher makes it fun to learn.

Hannah's mum says that once Hannah can read Braille it will make it easier for her to enjoy books and find out information. Hannah also uses a special machine called a **Braille embosser**, which can print out sheets in Braille. This means that if Hannah has to write a story for school, she can type it on her embosser and read it through.

*Opposite:* **Hannah told Sharon that the Braille alphabet is made up of six dots arranged in different patterns to represent each letter.**

**Hannah is learning how to read Braille and how to use her Braille embosser to make a page of Braille.**

## BLINDNESS FACTS

### COMPUTER HELP

Specially designed hardware and software can help visually impaired people who use Braille to get the most out of computer technology:

- Braille translation software enables a piece of printed text to be translated into Braille
- An electronic Braille display is a piece of equipment that displays a Braille version of the text that appears on a computer screen
- A Braille embosser can be connected to a computer in the same way as a printer to produce Braille instead of print on paper

# Staying over

*When Sharon stays at Hannah's for a sleepover the girls listen to music or a talking book before they go to bed.*

Sometimes Hannah asks me to describe what I can see or tell her how something looks. Because she has tunnel vision, she doesn't like things to be right in front of her face, so if I'm showing her something I have to hold it away from her a little.

Hannah has made me think more about the other senses I can use. When we went on a trip to the seaside, Hannah showed me what it was like to feel the weights and textures of the shells and pebbles on the beach. We listened to the rumble and crash of the waves on the shore. There were lots of different smells to take in, too.

Hannah and I get on really well. We spend time at each other's houses and we talk on the phone a lot. We help each other with any difficult homework, too. I'm glad we're friends.

*Hannah sometimes helps Sharon with her homework.*

# BLINDNESS FACTS

## SPORTS

Some of the sports which visually impaired people can take part in include:

- archery
- athletics
- cricket
- football
- goalball (a sport specially invented for visually impaired players)

- judo
- skiing
- swimming

# Out and about

*Hannah and her mum cross the road at a pedestrian crossing.*

Sometimes Hannah and I go to our local high street. We love to shop! Hannah's mum always comes with us to make sure Hannah's alright, but she lets Hannah do things for herself. I've noticed that Hannah uses all her senses to help her find out about what's around her. When she wants to pay for something, she

*Coins come in all shapes and sizes so that visually impaired people can tell them apart by feeling them.*

can tell which coins she needs by feeling them. When we're crossing a road, Hannah listens to the traffic sounds to make sure it has stopped and she waits for the signal which beeps to tell us it's safe to cross. Hannah told me that some blind people use a long **cane**, which they move from side to side, to let them know if there are any obstacles in their path. Hannah doesn't use a white cane at the moment, but her mum says she might decide to in the future.

## BLINDNESS FACTS

### HELPING OUT

Some ways in which you could help a visually impaired person in the street:

- Speak directly to the person and say who you are. Ask them if they would like any help and wait for them to tell you what sort of help they need (for example, they may need directions or help crossing the road)
- Let the person take your arm if you are guiding them. Tell them about any obstacles in good time and let them know if they are approaching a flight of steps or the edge of the pavement
- Say goodbye to let the person know you are leaving before you walk away

# Testing for problems

Hannah's mum told us about when she took Hannah to be seen by Mr Ronson, who is an ophthalmologist. An ophthalmologist is a doctor who specialises in treating eye diseases and problems. Hannah's mum told us what Mr Ronson did: 'If children are old enough, an ophthalmologist can ask them to read letters from a chart. But because Hannah was only two years old, Mr Ronson did something different. He held a teddy out in front of her face and then moved it away. He wanted to find out if Hannah would follow the teddy with her eyes. When she didn't, he knew that she had a problem with her sight.'

'After that he did some more tests and used special machinery to look into Hannah's eyes to find the cause of her problems. From his tests he was able to **diagnose** that Hannah had developed cancer of the retina in both her eyes. We later found out that there were cataracts in Hannah's eyes as well.'

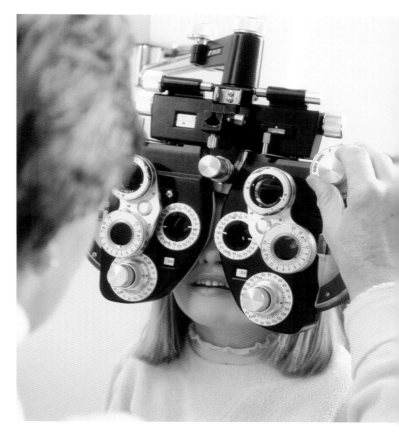

*Opposite:* **Hannah asks her mum lots of questions about when she was little.**

*An ophthalmologist examines a child's eyes.*

## BLINDNESS FACTS

### EYE TESTS

It's important for children and adults to have an eye test every two years. Regular checkups can identify any eye diseases or problems before they become too serious. The earlier a problem is treated, the greater the chance that it will not permanently damage a person's sight.

# Treating sight problems

*Hannah and her mum visit the hospital's eye clinic for regular eye checkups.*

Once Mr Ronson, the opthalmologist, had diagnosed Hannah's eye problem, he told her mum what could be done to help. Hannah's mum told us that doctors can correct some eye problems by prescribing glasses for the patient to wear.

Other eye problems, like Hannah's, need to be treated by surgery in a hospital. For example, an eye surgeon can operate on a patient to remove a lens that has been clouded by a cataract and replace it with an artificial lens. To cure Hannah's cancer, doctors had to remove her left eye, but were able to treat her right eye with **chemotherapy** and **radiotherapy**.

Hannah says she is glad that the doctors could treat her eyes and help her to see better, because some people's sight problems cannot be corrected. But Mr Ronson told Hannah's mum that everyone with a visual impairment, however it affects their vision, can get help to live independently and enjoy their lives.

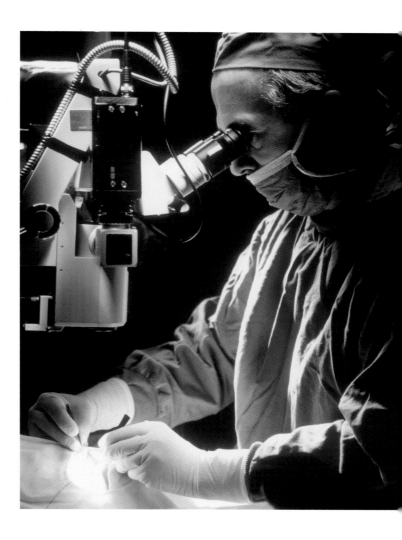

*An eye surgeon at work in the operating theatre of a hospital.*

# BLINDNESS FACTS

## SIGHT PROBLEMS

Some sight problems which children may have include:
- damage to their eyes as the result of an injury
- nystagmus – when the eyes move from side to side or up and down without the child controlling them
- retinoblastoma – the formation of cancerous tumours on the retina at the back of the eye
- visual impairment alongside other conditions, such as **epilepsy**

# In the park

Sometimes, Hannah and I go to the park after school. Her mum comes with us. Hannah and I love the park because there are big open areas of grass where we do handstands and cartwheels and run about. We like taking my dog Billy for a walk, too. Lots of people walk their dogs in the park.

We sometimes meet a lady called Mary, who is blind, walking with her **guide dog** Amber, who is a labrador.

Hannah explained to me that guide dogs are working dogs and we shouldn't interrupt Amber when she is working, in case she gets distracted. Mary says Amber is a very clever dog who's been trained to help her find her way around. She told us having a guide dog like Amber to help her has made her much more independent. Hannah cannot have a guide dog at the moment because she is too young and she still lives with her family.

*Opposite:* **Hannah and Sharon like to go to their local park.**

**Guide dogs help visually impaired people by guiding them along pavements and across roads.**

## BLINDNESS FACTS

### GUIDE DOGS

There are about 5000 visually impaired people in the UK who have guide dogs to help them at home and out in the street. Guide dogs are trained to help their owners by leading them around obstacles such as holes in the road, bicycles outside shops or chairs outside cafes. They are also trained to stop at the kerb and wait until their owner is ready to cross the road.

# Making the magazine

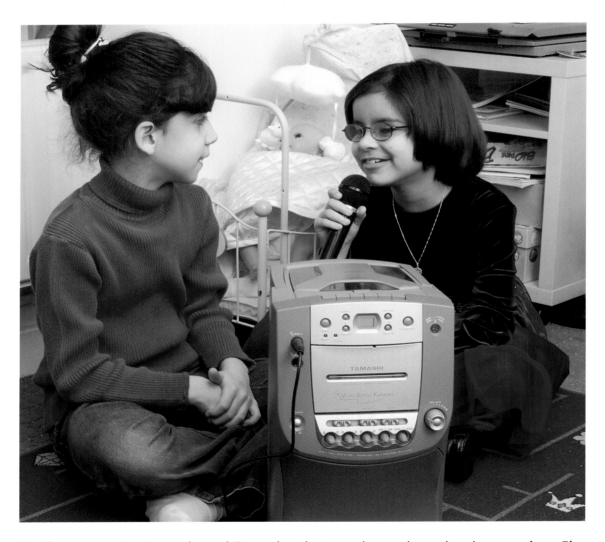

At the moment, Hannah and I are hard at work on the school magazine. I'm interviewing pupils to ask them what they would like to change about the school. Hannah is finding out about how schools in other countries provide for their disabled pupils.

Using the Internet, Hannah has got in touch with several children who are visually impaired from different countries around the world. She asked them what their lives are like at school. She's writing a report about what they said for the magazine. One boy told her he gets really fed up when people say he must have extra-sharp hearing because he can't see very well. He says his hearing's no better than average, he just listens more carefully to sounds around him. Someone else said it's very annoying when people don't speak directly to her – they talk to the person who's with her instead.

*Opposite:* **Hannah records her articles on her tape recorder before she types them up.**

**Hannah records an interview with a teacher for the school magazine.**

# BLINDNESS FACTS

## THE INTERNET

By connecting to the Internet via their computers, visually impaired people can have access to information and helpful advice from all over the world. Through email, they can communicate with others and discuss their experiences of being visually impaired. Schoolchildren can use the Internet to research information to help them with their studies.

# At school

*Hannah uses her talking computer to help her with her homework.*

There are other visually impaired children at our school and a few times a week they go to lessons which are specially designed for them. When Hannah started at school, her mum wrote to our headteacher to explain about her visual impairment and how the teachers could help. For example, Hannah's mum said that Hannah would find it easier to use a computer with a black screen as a background instead of a white one. As Hannah is **photosensitive**, a white screen can be too bright for her and make it uncomfortable to use the computer.

Hannah's computer is also fitted with speech software. When Hannah presses a key on the computer she can listen to what she has written.

Hannah enjoys herself at school. She is in the school orchestra and this year she's playing a solo on the piano at the end of term concert.

*Hannah has piano lessons and is learning ballet, too.*

# BLINDNESS FACTS

## TECHNOLOGY

There are several pieces of equipment that can help visually impaired children with their schoolwork:

- Word processors that can be programmed to enlarge the text that is shown on the screen up to 32 times its original size
- Screen-reader software which allows the text on the screen to be spoken aloud for the visually impaired user to hear
- Tapes and CDs which a visually impaired child can use to make a recording of something they need to learn, such as times tables, to play back as many times as they like

# Questions people ask

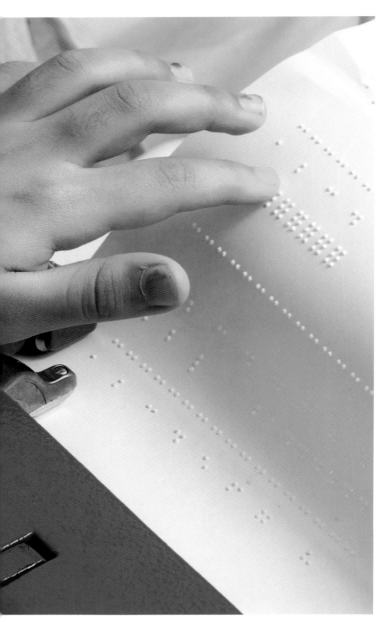

*A visually impaired person reads a sheet of Braille by running his or her finger across the bumps.*

Q. **What is it like to be blind?**
A. The experience of being visually impaired varies from one person to another. Some people are totally blind; some can tell the difference between darkness and light; others have blurred vision and cannot see things clearly. People like Hannah, who have tunnel vision, can see in front of them but not to the side, while other people may have no central vision. People who are visually impaired want to enjoy life and do the same things as sighted people – and they can, especially if they have help from people and equipment when they need it.

Q. **What job opportunities are there for visually impaired people?**
A. Visually impaired people are active in a range of careers, working, for example, in theatres, in offices and as computer programmers. Some visually impaired people take their guide dogs to the office with them.

Q. **Can visually impaired people enjoy films and television programmes?**
A. Yes they can, by listening to the

*Sharon and Hannah have now become close friends.*

soundtrack and having the scenery and action on screen described to them.

### Q. Is it difficult to learn Braille?

A. Generally, the older someone is when they lose their sight, the harder it is for them to learn Braille. Children find it easier, especially if, like Hannah, they have their own Braille teacher at school.

### Q. How can I help my friend who is visually impaired?

A. Ask your friend to let you know how you can help. For instance, Hannah likes her friends to switch on the light when she is in a room, so that she can see things more clearly. A visually impaired person may welcome your help in the street, for example, when crossing the road, but always introduce yourself first and ask if they would like any help.

*A blind person using a cane.*

# Glossary

**Braille** The reading and writing system used by visually impaired people that uses a combination of raised dots to represent letters and punctuation marks. It is named after its inventor, the Frenchman Louis Braille.

**Braille embosser** A machine that can produce sheets of Braille instead of normal print.

**cane** A stick which some visually impaired people use to let them know if there are any obstacles in their path. Sometimes visually impaired people use a foldaway cane which is called a symbol cane. This is used to show other people around them that they have problems with their sight.

**chemotherapy** A form of treatment for cancer that involves the use of chemicals.

**cornea** The see-through part of the eye's outer layer, at the front of the eye.

**developing countries** Countries in which many people are very poor and do not have enough food to eat, clean water to drink or an adequate healthcare system.

**diagnose** To identify a medical problem by considering someone's symptoms and the results of tests.

**epilepsy** An illness that affects the nervous system and causes people to have fits, during which they become unconscious.

**guide dog** A dog which has been trained to help a visually impaired person. It guides a person around obstacles.

**iris** A ring of muscles that forms the coloured part of the eye.

**lens** The curved part of the eye through which images are focused on the retina.

**nerves** The complicated network of fibres that carries messages to and from the brain and the other parts of the body.

**optic nerve** The nerve along which messages are sent from the eye to the brain.

**partially sighted** Having partial or incomplete sight. A person is said to be partially sighted if they cannot read the top line of an optician's eye chart from a distance of six metres or less.

**photosensitive** Finding bright light uncomfortable or painful.

**pupil** The hole in the centre of the iris.

**radiotherapy** A form of treatment for cancer that involves the use of radiation.

**retina** The inner lining of the eye.

**tunnel vision** Being able to see to the front, but not to the sides of the eyes.

**visual cortex** The area of the brain that processes signals from the eyes and works out what they mean.

**visual impairment** When a person's sight is limited in some way. Visual impairment has many causes and affects people in different ways.

# Useful organisations

**HERE ARE SOME ORGANISATIONS YOU MIGHT LIKE TO CONTACT FOR MORE INFORMATION ABOUT BLINDNESS AND VISUAL IMPAIRMENT**

**ACTION FOR BLIND PEOPLE**
14–16 Verney Road
London SE16 3DZ
Tel: 020 7635 4800
Information and advice service helpline:
0800 915 4666
email: info@afbp.org
**www.afbp.org**

**BRITISH BLIND SPORT**
4–6 Victoria Terrace
Leamington Spa
Warwickshire CV31 3AB
Tel: 08700 789000
email: info@britishblindsport.org.uk
**www.britishblindsport.org.uk**

**THE GUIDE DOGS FOR THE BLIND ASSOCIATION**
Burghfield Common
Reading RG7 3YG
Tel: 0870 600 2323
email: guidedogs@guidedogs.org.uk
**www.guidedogs.org.uk**

Related website: **www.healthyeyes.org.uk**

**ROYAL NATIONAL INSTITUTE OF THE BLIND**
224 Great Portland Street
London W1N 6AA
Tel: 020 7388 1266
Helpline: 0845 766 9999
**www.rnib.org.uk**

# Index